SODA FOUNTAIN
Classics

ICE CREAM, SUNDAES, MILKSHAKES, AND MORE

Elsa Petersen-Schepelern PHOTOGRAPHY BY *Debi Treloar*

RYLAND
PETERS
& SMALL
LONDON NEW YORK

Senior Designer	Louise Leffler
Designer	Victoria Holmes
Design assistant	Luis Peral-Aranda
Editor	Maddalena Bastianelli
Production	Patricia Harrington
Head of Design	Gabriella Le Grazie
Publishing Director	Anne Ryland
Food Stylist	Maxine Clark
Stylist	Wei Tang
Photographer's Assistant	Lina Ikse Bergman

Acknowledgements

My thanks to my sister Kirsten and to Peter Bray.
Thanks also to Wei Tang for her inspired props, Maxine Clarke for her endless good humour and wicked food styling (and for donating her amazing cookie recipe), my friend Maddie Bastianelli (the "Baking Queen") for her help with recipe testing, Louise Leffler for her lush design, and to Debi Treloar for her wonderful photographs.
Particular thanks to Debi's husband Colin and her sons Woody and Quinn, for their enthusiastic road-testing of the recipes in this book. Thanks also to Randal Mar of Magdalene House Designs, Langthorne, in North Yorkshire for his beautiful wooden ice cream cone mold, hand-turned especially for this book.

First published in the USA in 2000

10 9 8 7 6 5 4

by Ryland Peters & Small
519 Broadway, 5th Floor, New York, NY 10012

Text © Elsa Petersen-Schepelern 2000
Design and photographs © Ryland Peters & Small 2000
Photographs pages 6–9 © Hulton Getty Images
Photographs pages 11, 20–21, 28–29 by Sandra Lane

Printed and bound in China

ISBN 1 84172 046 1

Notes

All spoon measurements are level unless otherwise stated.

Ice creams in this book were made using a Waring Blender and Musso Piccolo electric ice cream maker. If you don't have a churn, ice cream may be put in shallow freezer boxes, partially frozen, then broken up with a fork or food processor. Partially freeze again, then crush or blend again. Repeat at least once more—the more often you do this, the better the final texture. The ice cream may then be frozen until ready to serve, but serve it as soon as possible. Though still safe to eat, the texture will suffer the longer you leave it.

Contents

INTRODUCTION

In our town, there was a wonderful ice cream parlor—
all leadlight glass, polished banquettes, and enough ice
cream sundaes to make any little girl's eyes pop.

My elegant mother, dressed in hat and gloves and
what was then called the "New Look," would order
waffles with syrup and ice cream. I would have a
sundae—not just any ice cream, but utterly over-the-top
ice cream. With nuts, and wafers like jaunty sails, and
sweet colored syrups pooling around the ice cream.

Dinner party triumphs   Since then, I have found that
serving sundaes at a dinner party brings great *oohs* and
aahs of delight, as guests suddenly remember their
childhood visits to the ice cream parlor. Grown men ask
for seconds after having downed a banana split in
record time. And some people, when faced with
chocolate anything, become utterly irrational.

How sundaes got their name   Amazing as it may
seem, late last century, sodas were seen as too exciting
to be served on a Sunday, the Lord's day—it was feared
by community busybodies that the fizz would whip the

female population into a frenzy of desire. But an enterprising entrepreneur saved the day—he served ice cream instead and the "sundae" was born. (Personally, I think that ice cream is much more thrilling than soda.)

Soda fountain success Not so long ago, no respectable woman would have been seen dead in a bar, while last century she wouldn't even go to a restaurant. But the soda fountain and ice cream parlor have always been respectable, and hugely popular with women and girls (and with possible suitors).

Though everyone loves ice cream, some countries make it better than others. Italy produces marvelous ice cream, as does India (not surprising, since the cow is sacred) and Denmark, which is one of the world's top dairy producing countries. But, perhaps the greatest ice cream nation of all is America—and we owe it all to Prohibition. During the Twenties and early Thirties, when alcohol was banned across the States (and incidentally, booze consumption sky-rocketed) the breweries found themselves out of work. So, to keep their companies running, they turned to the ice cream business instead.

Making ice cream You can make ice cream sundaes and sodas using any good-quality ice cream from your supermarket, but it's much better to make your own to ensure the freshest taste, best flavor, and highest quality.

I use an electric ice cream maker to make my ice cream, and they are reasonably inexpensive these days. (In fact, I share mine with several friends.) But, if you don't have one, you can still make ice cream using an ordinary freezer. Pour the mixture into shallow freezer boxes and partially freeze until crystals have formed around the edges. Take the mixture out of the boxes and blend in a food processor or beat with a fork. Freeze again. Repeat this at least once more, though the more often you do it the more perfect the texture of the ice cream will be.

Old-fashioned nostalgia Summertime used to mean sitting in an ice cream parlor or soda fountain, sipping a chocolate milkshake or a strawberry malted, eating delicious spoonfuls from a dish of sherbet or ice cream sundae. The recipes in this book will help you remember these wonderful classic American treats.

Above: The soda fountain, ice cream parlor, and drugstore were the natural home of the sundae and the soda.
Previous page: Soda fountains weren't just for children—this one was a favorite haunt of hard-bitten journalists.

Knickerbocker glory

1 tablespoon chocolate sauce*

2 scoops vanilla ice cream

about 3–4 tablespoons fresh
raspberries, crushed with a fork

1 scoop strawberry ice cream

1–2 tablespoons chopped fresh fruit,
such as pineapple or apricots

about 1–2 tablespoons
whipped cream

about 1 teaspoon toasted almonds,
coarsely crushed

1 maraschino cherry

SERVES 1

Sauces and syrups pages 56–61

A WONDERFULLY INDULGENT AND NOSTALGIC SUNDAE, WHICH IS ONE OF THE MOST DELICIOUS OF ALL.

Carefully spoon the chocolate syrup into the bottom of a tall soda glass. Add 1 scoop vanilla ice cream, then about 1 tablespoon crushed fresh raspberries.

Add 1 scoop strawberry ice cream, then a layer of chopped fresh pineapple or apricots. Add another scoop of vanilla and another layer of crushed berries. Top with a big cloud of whipped cream and sprinkle with toasted almonds and a cherry.

Put 2 straws and a long parfait spoon into the glass and serve.

Sundaes & Parfaits

TRY SUNDAES IN FLAT DISHES OR
PARFAITS IN TALL GLASSES—WITH
HOMEMADE OR STORE-BOUGHT ICE
CREAM PLUS DELICIOUS SAUCES,
SYRUPS, AND TOPPINGS.

Banana split

1 ripe banana

3 scoops ice cream, one each of vanilla, chocolate, and strawberry

1 tablespoon chocolate sauce*

1 tablespoon butterscotch sauce*

1 tablespoon strawberry sauce*

2–4 tablespoons whipped cream

1 tablespoon crushed mixed nuts

2–3 maraschino cherries

2 wafers, to serve (optional)

SERVES 1

Sauces and syrups pages 56–61

THE GRANDDADDY OF ALL SUNDAES—AN AMERICAN CLASSIC, JUST DRIPPING WITH CHOCOLATE. IT HARKENS BACK TO THE DAYS WHEN BANANAS WERE A SPECIAL TREAT RATHER THAN AN EVERYDAY FRUIT.

Cut the banana in half lengthwise and put it in a long, shallow, glass dish. Put 3 scoops ice cream, in different flavors, down the length of the banana, between the 2 halves, and sitting up above them. Drizzle the 3 sauces over the top. Spoon the cream around the base of the dish and over the ice cream. Sprinkle the sundae with chopped nuts and top with the cherries. If using wafers, set them in the ice cream at a jaunty angle.

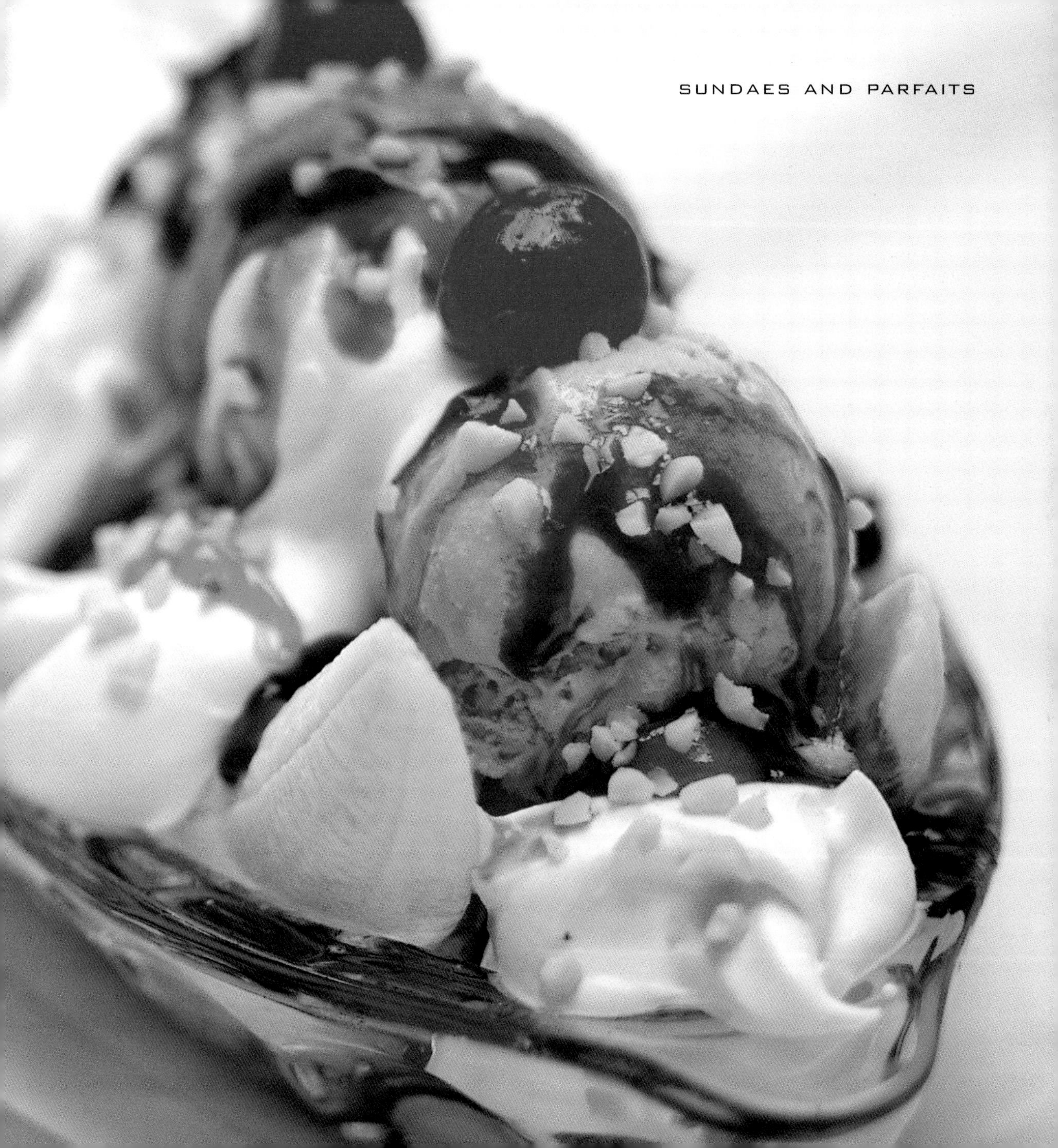

HOT SAUCES MAKE A DELICIOUS
CONTRAST WITH COLD ICE CREAM.
THIS ONE IS BUTTERSCOTCH, BUT
I ALSO LOVE CARAMEL, RUM-RAISIN,
OR HOT FUDGE (PAGE 16).

3 scoops very cold chocolate
or vanilla ice cream

1 scoop very cold
coffee or vanilla ice cream

¼ cup hot butterscotch sauce*

nut brittle (page 48) or
toasted nuts, very cold

SERVES 1

*Sauces and syrups pages 56–61

Use a metal sundae dish or thick, heatproof glass bowl, so it won't be cracked by the hot sauce. Put 3 scoops chocolate or vanilla ice cream in the base and balance 1 scoop coffee or vanilla ice cream on top. Spoon half the hot butterscotch sauce around the ice cream.

Pour the remaining sauce over the top, sprinkle with nut brittle or toasted nuts, then serve.

VARIATION:

Hot Rum-Raisin Sundae Pour warm rum-raisin sauce (page 58) over vanilla ice cream.

Hot butterscotch sundae

Fudge sauce sundae

FUDGE—WHETHER HOT OR COLD—IS ONE OF THE GREAT SODA FOUNTAIN CLASSICS. POUR HOT FUDGE SAUCE OVER THIS INDULGENT COMBINATION OF FRUIT AND ICE CREAM, OR THE SIMPLER VERSION ON THE PREVIOUS PAGE, WITH OR WITHOUT NUTS.

3 scoops very cold vanilla ice cream

1 tablespoon yellow fruit syrup, such as pineapple or apricot*

1 apricot, fresh or canned, sliced (optional)

3 tablespoons stiffly whipped cream

2 tablespoons cold strawberry sauce*

2–3 tablespoons hot fudge sauce*

1–2 fan-shaped wafers

SERVES 1

*Sauces and syrups pages 56–61

Put 1 scoop of the ice cream in a heatproof sundae glass, then add the yellow fruit syrup and sliced apricot, if using. Add the whipped cream, then the strawberry sauce. Add the remaining 2 scoops of vanilla ice cream.

Spoon the hot fudge sauce over the top, then serve topped with 1–2 fan-shaped ice cream wafers.

VARIATION:

Hot Caramel Sundae Layer scoops of chocolate, vanilla, and caramel ice cream in a glass and pour caramel sauce (page 60) over the top.

All Chocolate Sundae Fill the glass with chocolate ice cream and whipped cream, then top with hot fudge sauce and fan-shaped wafers.

17

To make the praline, put the pecans in a dry skillet or on a baking tray in a preheated oven at 400°F. Toast until golden brown. Remove the pecans from the heat and rub in a clean cloth to remove some of the papery skins.

Put the sugar in a food processor with the vanilla bean and process until the bean has been ground to a speckled powder.

Put the vanilla sugar in a saucepan with ½ cup water and dissolve over high heat. The sugar will bubble and begin to turn brown. When it is a rich gold, add the pecans and stir for 1 minute. Spread the mixture onto a greased baking sheet. Let cool. Break up the praline into large pieces with a rolling pin and transfer to a food processor. Process until crumbly, then remove any large pieces. Pour the rest into the ice cream mixture and churn.

Break or coarsely chop the remaining large pieces of praline into smaller pieces. Reserve for decoration.

To serve, put a spoonful of whipped cream in a tall parfait glass or sundae dish, add a scoop of praline ice cream, then top with lots of maple syrup. Sprinkle with the reserved praline (and more crushed pecans, if preferred).

PRALINE IS A MIXTURE OF NUTS AND CARAMEL, WHICH IS THEN CRUSHED OR GROUND INTO A COARSE MEAL. IT IS A SOUTHERN SPECIALITY AND IS OFTEN MADE WITH ALMONDS, BUT WHEN MADE WITH PECANS, AS HERE, IT IS TYPICALLY NEW ORLEANS.

1 recipe vanilla
ice cream (page 43)

4 tablespoons
whipped cream

½ cup maple syrup

crushed toasted
pecans, to serve
(optional)

Praline:

1 cup pecans, about 4 oz.

1¼ cups sugar

1 inch piece of vanilla bean

1 baking sheet, greased

SERVES 4

Praline parfait

Fresh fruit sundae

Put the crushed fruit in a shallow dish, sprinkle with the sugar, and set aside for 15 minutes. Lightly fold the vanilla through the whipped cream. When ready to serve, put 1 large scoop ice cream into a coupe-style ice cream dish or tall soda glass. Add a large spoonful of the crushed fruit and a second scoop of ice cream. Pile the whipped cream on top, sprinkle with nuts, top with maraschino cherries, if using, and serve with a fan-shaped wafer.

about ½ cup crushed fresh fruit, such as berries or pineapple

1 tablespoon sugar or confectioner's sugar

1 drop pure vanilla extract

2 heaping tablespoons whipped cream

2 large scoops vanilla ice cream

1 tablespoon crushed nuts

1–2 maraschino cherries (optional)

1 fan-shaped wafer

SERVES 1

IN SUMMER, WHEN FRESH FRUIT IS IN ABUNDANCE,
THIS SUNDAE—MADE WITH SWEET STRAWBERRIES
OR RIPE APRICOTS—IS A DELICIOUS TREAT.

Peach sundae

A PEACH MELBA-GONE-SUNDAE. YOU WILL LOVE THE POACHED PEACHES, SO MAKE A LARGE QUANTITY AND SERVE ANY EXTRAS WITH HEAVY CREAM AND A SPOONFUL OF THE BEAUTIFUL JUICE. CHOOSE RED-SKINNED FRUIT WITH YELLOW FLESH FOR BEST COLOR.

½ cup whipping cream

1 tablespoon confectioner's sugar

4 scoops vanilla ice cream

¼ cup raspberry sauce*

Poached Peaches:

4 peaches, halved and pitted, but not peeled

¼ cup sugar

1 inch vanilla bean, split lengthwise

To serve (optional):

fresh raspberries

crushed nuts

lady fingers or other wafers*

SERVES 4

*Sauces and syrups pages 56–61
Cones and wafers pages 52–55

To poach the peaches, put them in a small stainless steel saucepan with the sugar and piece of vanilla bean. Cover with water, bring to a boil, then simmer until tender, about 10–15 minutes. Cool and chill, still in their skins, which will lend color to the fruit. Keep in the poaching syrup. When ready to serve, pinch off and discard the skins (they come off easily).

To whip the cream, put it in a bowl, sprinkle with the confectioner's sugar, then beat until soft peaks form.

Put two peach halves in a sundae dish, set open like the leaves of a book. Put a scoop of vanilla ice cream between the 2 halves. Spoon some of the peach poaching syrup around, then add a spoonful of raspberry sauce.

Serve plain or sprinkle with raspberries and nuts, add the lady fingers or wafers, and serve with whipped cream.

23

Romanov parfait

Rinse the strawberries, pat dry with paper towels and reserve 4 of the best berries for decoration. Hull and halve the remainder (always rinse before hulling, not after, or the strawberries will fill with water). Put the cut berries in a bowl, sprinkle with the liqueur and 1 tablespoon of the confectioner's sugar, and set aside for 30 minutes. Whip the cream with the vanilla and the remaining sugar until firm peaks form. Cover and chill until ready to use.
To serve, spoon the berries into small glass dishes, top with ice cream, whipped cream, and a reserved strawberry, halved.

1 basket strawberries, about 8 oz.

2 tablespoons orange-flavor liqueur, such as Cointreau, Grand Marnier, or Triple Sec

1½ tablespoons confectioner's sugar

½ cup heavy cream

a few drops of vanilla extract

4–8 scoops strawberry or vanilla ice cream

SERVES 4

STRAWBERRIES ROMANOV
IS A CLASSIC FRENCH
DISH. THIS IS A SUNDAE
VERSION OF THE ORIGINAL,
ELEGANT ENOUGH FOR A
DINNER PARTY.

Layered ice cream sundae

2–3 scoops ice cream,
vanilla or fruit flavored

fruit such as sliced poached peaches
(page 24), crushed pineapple,
raspberries, sliced fresh strawberries,
bananas, or passionfruit pulp

2 tablespoons whipped cream

strawberry sauce or other fruit
syrup*

your choice of toppings, to serve*

SERVES 1

*Sauces and syrups pages 56–61
Toppings pages 62–63

YOUR FAVORITE SUNDAE— USE ANY COMBINATION OF FAVORITE INGREDIENTS.

In a tall soda glass, put a scoop of ice cream, a
layer of fruit, a layer of whipped cream, another
scoop of ice cream, a second layer of fruit, more
ice cream, more cream, and more fruit.
Drizzle with strawberry sauce or other fruit syrup.
Add your choice of toppings such as crushed nuts,
jimmies, or toasted coconut.

Waffle hearts

Serve ice cream and syrup on top of the waffles, or make hearts for a special occasion.

Waffle Batter:

1⅔ cups all-purpose flour

¼ teaspoon salt

1½ teaspoons baking powder

2 eggs, separated

1 cup milk

1 tablespoon butter, melted

To serve:

2 cups strawberry ice cream

½ cup strawberry sauce*

confectioner's sugar, for dusting

an electric 4-heart-patterned waffle iron, greased

a heart-shaped cookie cutter

SERVES 4

*Sauces and syrups pages 56–61

To make the waffle batter, sift the flour, salt, and baking powder into a bowl and make a well in the center. Beat the egg yolks until creamy. Beat the egg whites in a second bowl until stiff and frothy. Pour the melted butter into the flour, then the egg yolks and milk. Mix well, then fold in the beaten egg whites.

Heat the waffle iron until faintly smoking. Pour a little batter into each compartment and spread over quickly. Close the waffle iron and leave for 1 minute until golden brown. Transfer the waffle to a heated plate and cook the remaining mixture in the same way. Break the waffles into the heart segments.

Using the cookie cutter, make a 1½-inch thick strawberry ice cream heart. Put a waffle heart on a chilled plate, add an ice cream heart, and top with a second waffle heart. Drizzle with strawberry sauce and dust with confectioner's sugar.

Note: Cooked waffles can be kept in a warm oven for about 20 minutes. Waffles can be frozen, then reheated from frozen in a preheated oven at 350°F for 10 minutes.

$\mathcal{B}$lack cow

1½ tablespoons chocolate sauce*
or store-bought syrup

about 1¼ cups root beer

2 scoops vanilla ice cream

SERVES 1

Sauces and syrups pages 56–61

Put the chocolate sauce or syrup in the bottom of a large ice cream soda glass. Add half the root beer and mix well with a long soda spoon. Add 1 scoop ice cream, then top up the glass with the remaining root beer.

Traditionally, the remaining scoop of ice cream is balanced on the rim of the glass—press it down firmly so it doesn't dive onto the table.

VARIATION:

Brown Cow Substitute cola for the root beer.

THIS CLASSIC ICE FLOAT IS PURE NOSTALGIA FOR THE TRUE ICE CREAM PARLOR LOVER. ROOT BEER MAKES THE COW BLACK, COLA MAKES HER BROWN.

SODAS & MALTEDS

YOU CAN RECREATE NOSTALGIC
MEMORIES OF SODA FOUNTAIN
MALTEDS, SODAS, AND EGG
CREAMS USING YOUR FAVORITE
ICE CREAM AND SYRUPS.

ONE OF NEW YORK'S GREAT
CONTRIBUTIONS TO THE SODA
FOUNTAIN REPERTOIRE—WHICH,
INTERESTINGLY, CONTAINS NEITHER
EGGS NOR CREAM.

New York egg cream

2 tablespoons chocolate syrup

milk (see recipe)

seltzer, to serve

SERVES 1

Put the chocolate syrup in a tall soda glass, fill ⅓ of the glass with milk. Stir with a long spoon. Top with the seltzer and serve—the top should be very frothy.

Note: Fox's U-Bet is the traditional chocolate syrup for an egg cream. If you don't have access to it, use another brand such as Hershey's or Bosco.

33

Favorite floats

1 large scoop ice cream,
such as vanilla, raspberry,
or strawberry

1 small bottle flavored soda,
such as lime, raspberry,
strawberry, or cherry

SERVES 1

Put the ice cream in the bottom of a tall soda glass. Add a parfait spoon and straws. Serve on a small saucer, with a bottle of raspberry, strawberry, or cherry soda beside. Each person adds soda, stirring the ice cream into the mix if preferred.

VARIATIONS:

Pineapple Float Use vanilla or pineapple ice cream with pineapple soda.

Old-Fashioned Float For that old-time flavor, instead of berry or cherry soda, use plain soda plus a spoonful of fruit syrup (page 61).

35

Put the milk in a blender with the vanilla syrup, malted milk powder, and ice cream. Blend until frothy. Serve in the metal container, with a separate soda glass, straws, and parfait spoons.

VARIATIONS:

Strawberry Malted Omit the vanilla and substitute red berry sauce (page 61). Use either vanilla or strawberry ice cream.

Chocolate Malted Omit the vanilla and substitute chocolate syrup. You can use either vanilla or chocolate ice cream.

Caramel Malted Omit the vanilla and substitute caramel sauce (page 60). Use either vanilla or chocolate ice cream.

1 cup milk

2 teaspoons vanilla syrup*

1 teaspoon malted milk powder

2 scoops vanilla ice cream

SERVES 1

To make vanilla syrup, put 1 part sugar to 3 parts water in a saucepan and heat gently until the sugar dissolves and the mixture becomes a light syrup. Stir in a few drops vanilla extract, then bottle, seal, and store in the refrigerator for use in drinks, cocktails, and desserts. Alternatively, use commercial vanilla syrup.

Malted milk shakes

Much as I adore malteds, I must warn that they are deliciously fattening. Have them as a special treat, or omit the malt and have a milkshake instead. If you actually need to put on weight, there can be no more delicious medicine.

Vanilla milkshake

SODA FOUNTAINS OFTEN WRAPPED
THE METAL MILKSHAKE CONTAINER IN A
NAPKIN SO LADIES WOULDN'T STAIN THEIR
GLOVES. THE SAME LADIES WOULD FIND
MILKSHAKES LESS WAISTLINE-CHALLENGING
THAN MALTEDS, AND MODERN LOW-FAT MILK
WILL BE LESS ALARMING TO THE DIET-
CONSCIOUS. YOU CAN BUY DRINK MIXER
MACHINES BASED ON THE OLD SODA
FOUNTAIN CLASSICS—OR USE A BLENDER
INSTEAD. CRUSHED ICE WILL MAKE THE
DRINK FROTH MORE.

1 cup milk

2 teaspoons vanilla syrup (page 36)

1 scoop vanilla ice cream

SERVES 1

Put all the ingredients in a blender or drink mixer and blend until frothy. Transfer to a metal milkshake container and serve separately in a tall soda glass with a saucer, napkins, straws, and a long parfait spoon.

VARIATIONS:

Chocolate Milkshake Instead of the vanilla syrup, use 1 tablespoon chocolate sauce (page 58) or chocolate syrup.

Caramel Milkshake Omit the vanilla syrup. Add 1 teaspoon caramel sauce (page 60) or syrup.

Banana Milkshake Omit the vanilla. Slice half a banana into a blender with the ice cream, 1 teaspoon simple syrup, and half the milk. Blend until smooth, then add the remaining milk. Blend and serve with an extra scoop of ice cream on top.

Pineapple Milkshake Omit the vanilla syrup, add ¼ cup pineapple syrup (page 61) and proceed as in the main recipe.

39

WHENEVER YOU SQUEEZE FRUIT JUICE, POUR SOME INTO
ICE CUBE TRAYS AND FREEZE FOR LATER.

Fruit frappé

2 cups freshly squeezed fruit juice,
such as apple, raspberry, pineapple
or other juice

SERVES 2

Freeze the juice in ice cube trays. When ready to
serve, transfer to a food processor and process in
short bursts until crushed but not slushy.
Alternatively, put the ice cubes in the refrigerator for
a couple of minutes to soften a little, then mash
them with a fork. Serve in chilled glasses.

40

Iced coffee

½ cup strong espresso coffee, cooled
and chilled, or 2 tablespoons coffee
syrup (page 60)

1 cup milk or cream

1 scoop vanilla ice cream

To serve (optional):

1–2 tablespoons whipped cream

1 coffee bean, crushed, to serve

sugar, to taste

SERVES 1

Put the coffee into a blender with the milk or cream and ice cream, if using. Blend until smooth, then serve topped with a swirl of whipped cream and a sprinkle of crushed coffee bean, if using. Serve sugar separately and sweeten to taste.

VARIATION

Iced Coffee Viennese Make the iced coffee as in the main recipe, stir in 1 tablespoon rum or brandy, then top with whipped cream.

Ice creams

Ice creams from the great days of the soda fountain were intensely rich. I include three basic recipes, with classic flavors like vanilla, caramel, chocolate, strawberry, and so on, plus the new "exotics" like pineapple. Modern tastes like mango just aren't authentic (but try them if you like).

Vanilla ice cream

THIS BASIC ICE CREAM RECIPE CAN BE PUT TOGETHER IN
HALF AN HOUR AND FLAVORED IN LOTS OF DIFFERENT
WAYS. MAKE SURE ALL THE INGREDIENTS ARE WELL
CHILLED, THEN MIX AND CHURN. EASY! OMIT THE
GELATIN IF YOU LIKE, BUT IT DOES GIVE GOOD TEXTURE.

Mix the milk, sugar, and condensed milk in a blender until the sugar dissolves. Alternatively, dissolve the

sugar in 2 tablespoons hot water (microwave in 10-second bursts if preferred). Let cool a little, then add

to the blender with the cream, vanilla, and salt. Blend briefly. Add any flavorings, then chill.

If using gelatin, dissolve according to the package instructions. Add to the mixture. Churn and freeze.

2 cups milk

¼ cup sugar

½ cup condensed milk
(half a small can)

½ cup heavy cream

2 teaspoons vanilla extract

a pinch of salt

1 tablespoon gelatin
(optional)

MAKES 4 CUPS

Flavorings—your choice of:

1 cup strawberry sauce*
or other fruit purée

1 cup coffee syrup*

3 oz. peppermint candies,
crushed in a food processor and
2 tablespoons peppermint syrup

1 cup pineapple syrup*

*Sauces and syrups pages 56–61

Rich Vanilla Ice Cream

3 eggs, plus 2–3 yolks

4 cups milk or light cream

1¼ cups sugar

MAKES ABOUT 6 CUPS

Put the eggs and yolks in a bowl and beat until smooth.

Heat the milk (or cream) and sugar in a saucepan to just below boiling.

Gradually stir ½ cup of the hot liquid into the beaten eggs, then stir the mixture back into the saucepan. Stir over a gentle heat until the mixture thickens (stir in the same direction). Do not let it boil or the custard will curdle. (Some people use a double boiler or a bowl set over a saucepan of simmering water). When the mixture is thick enough to coat the back of a spoon, remove from the heat, strain into a bowl or pitcher, cool, and chill. Churn (in batches if necessary) and freeze.

VARIATIONS:

Flavorings should be added just before churning. They include:

Rich Strawberry Ice Cream

Add 1 cup mashed fresh strawberries or ½ cup strawberry sauce (page 61).

Rich Chocolate Ice Cream

Melt 4–5 squares unsweetened chocolate in a heatproof bowl set over simmering water. Alternatively, microwave at medium in short 30-second bursts (about 2 minutes in all) until melted. Stir a little of the Rich Vanilla Ice Cream mixture into the chocolate, then stir the chocolate back into the custard. Churn and freeze.

Alternatively, add 3 extra squares of chocolate, grated or worked in a blender, before churning.

Rich Caramel Ice Cream Omit the sugar from the main recipe. Stir in 1 quantity caramel sauce (page 60), churn, and freeze.

Rich Coffee Ice Cream Stir in ½ cup coffee syrup (page 60), then churn and freeze.

Note: If you don't have an ice cream maker, partially freeze the mixture. Blend in a food processor until smooth. Alternatively, beat with a fork. Refreeze.

If you repeat the freezing and processing several times, the mixture will be smoother.

Custard-based ice creams

ADAPT THESE RECIPES TO SUIT THE CAPACITY OF
YOUR ICE CREAM MACHINE—OR YOUR APPETITE.
TAKE CARE WITH THE QUANTITY OF SUGAR USED. IF
TOO LITTLE, IT WILL TAKE A LONG TIME TO FREEZE.
IF TOO MUCH, IT WON'T FREEZE AT ALL. REMEMBER
THAT THE FLAVORING ELEMENT (ESPECIALLY CARAMEL)
WILL OFTEN CONTAIN SUGAR, SO REDUCE THE SUGAR
CONTENT OF THE CUSTARD ACCORDINGLY.

Sherbets and ice milks

SODA FOUNTAIN SHERBETS WERE A MIXTURE OF MILK AND FRUIT JUICE OR WATER. DATING BACK TO THE DEPRESSION ERA, THEY CONTAIN LESS FAT THAN ICE CREAM, SO ARE ALMOST MODERN IN THEIR APPROACH.

Raspberry sherbet

3 cups raspberries, fresh or frozen

1 cup sugar

juice of 1 lemon

2 cups very cold milk

MAKES ABOUT 4–5 CUPS

Mix the raspberries, sugar, and lemon juice in a blender. Add half the milk and blend until the sugar dissolves. Add the remaining milk and blend again. Churn, in batches if necessary, and serve.

Pineapple sherbet

1 cup fresh pineapple, puréed, or pineapple juice or other fruit juice

1 cup sugar

½ cup fresh lemon juice (2–3 lemons)

a pinch of salt

2 cups very cold milk

MAKES ABOUT 4–5 CUPS

Mix the pineapple purée or juice, sugar, lemon juice, and salt in a blender. Let stand for a few minutes, then blend again. When the sugar has dissolved, add the milk and blend again. Churn and serve.

Lemon sherbet

1 cup sugar

grated zest and juice of 1 lemon

1 cup very cold milk

MAKES ABOUT 3 CUPS

Put the sugar, lemon zest, and 1 cup water in a saucepan and heat until the sugar dissolves. Chill. Stir in the lemon juice. Pour the milk into the ice cream maker, then add the lemon water. Churn and serve.

Nut brittle ice cream

1 recipe vanilla ice cream
(page 43 or 44)

3 squares unsweetened chocolate ,
chopped

Nut Brittle:

6 tablespoons sugar

½ cup pecans or almonds,
coarsely crushed

peanut or corn oil, for brushing

1 baking sheet, greased

SERVES 4

Put the sugar and 6 tablespoons
water in a saucepan, stir, then
bring to a boil over medium heat.
Continue boiling until golden
brown. Add the nuts, pour onto
the baking sheet, let cool, and set.
When set, break up the brittle,
then crush with a rolling pin.
Make the ice cream (or slightly

soften some you made earlier).
Microwave the chocolate at
medium in 30-second bursts
(about 2 minutes in all) until
melted. Alternatively, melt in a
double boiler over simmering
water. Cool the chocolate, then
stir it and the crushed brittle into
the ice cream. Freeze again.
Soften in the refrigerator for
15 minutes before serving.

Rocky road

1 recipe chocolate ice cream
(page 43 or 44)

1 recipe nut brittle (see previous
recipe, left)

1½ cups mini marshmallows

SERVES 4

Make the ice cream and, just
before churning is finished, add
the nut brittle. Let churn 5 more

minutes, then transfer to a
plastic container and stir in the
marshmallows until evenly
distributed. Freeze. Serve with
extras such as chopped nuts,
shaved chocolate, and nut brittle.

Mint chocolate chip

1 recipe vanilla or chocolate
ice cream (page 43 or 44)

about 4 oz. chocolate mints, frozen

SERVES 4

Put the mints in a food
processor and blend coarsely.
Stir into freshly churned ice
cream. Alternatively, churn the
ice cream with half the
chocolate mints, then stir in the
remainder and freeze.

Delicious combinations

Chocolate chip cookie ice cream sandwiches

6 tablespoons unsalted butter, softened

6 tablespoons sugar

6 tablespoons brown sugar, sifted

1 large egg, beaten

½ teaspoon vanilla extract

1 cup self-rising flour

¼ cup unsweetened cocoa powder

¼ teaspoon salt

⅔ cup chocolate chips (semisweet, milk, or white), or coarsely chopped chocolate

vanilla ice cream, for filling

several non-stick baking sheets, lightly greased

MAKES 6 SANDWICHES

Cream the butter and sugars together until pale and fluffy.

Beat in the egg and vanilla.

Sift the flour, cocoa, and salt into a bowl, then fold into the egg mixture. Fold in the chocolate morsels.

Put 4 heaping tablespoons of the mixture spaced well apart on each baking sheet. Press them down and spread them out using the back of a wet spoon.

Bake in a preheated oven at 350°F for 12–15 minutes. Remove from the oven, let cool on the baking sheet for 1 minute, then remove to a wire rack. When cold, use immediately or store in an airtight container for up to 5 days.

To assemble the sandwiches, spread a thick (about 1 inch) layer of ice cream on a cookie, then press a second one on top. Repeat until all the sandwiches are made, then freeze until ready to serve.

Ice cream cones

Plain Ice Cream Cones:

¾ cup confectioner's sugar

5 tablespoons unsalted butter, softened

4 egg whites, beaten

1 cup plus 2 tablespoons all-purpose flour

1 teaspoon cornstarch

Pizzelle Cones:

3 eggs

¾ cup sugar

1 stick butter, melted and cooled

1 teaspoon vanilla extract

1¾ cups all-purpose flour

2 teaspoons baking powder

non-stick baking sheets or an electric Italian pizelle maker

wooden cone-mold

MAKES ABOUT 30

To make plain cones, sift the confectioner's sugar into a bowl. Add the butter and mix with a wooden spoon. Using an electric beater, beat until pale and light. Beat in the egg whites, a little at a time. Mix the flour with the cornstarch, then sift into the bowl and fold in until smooth. Using a spatula, spread the batter thinly into 4-inch circles on the baking sheets. Bake in a preheated oven at 375°F for 6–8 minutes. Remove from the baking sheet with a spatula and curl around the cone mold*. Let cool then remove and cool completely. Use immediately or store in an airtight container for up to 5 days.

If using a pizelle maker, beat the eggs and sugar until pale, then stir in the butter and vanilla. Sift the flour and baking powder together, then stir into the egg mixture. Prepare the pizelle maker according to the manufacturer's instructions, then put 1 teaspoon batter in the middle of each section. Close the lid and cook for 30 seconds until golden. Remove with a spatula and shape around a cone mold as before*. Cool and store as for plain ice cream cones.

*Note: If you can't find the special wooden cone mold shown here, use any other cone, such as a cream horn mold, instead.

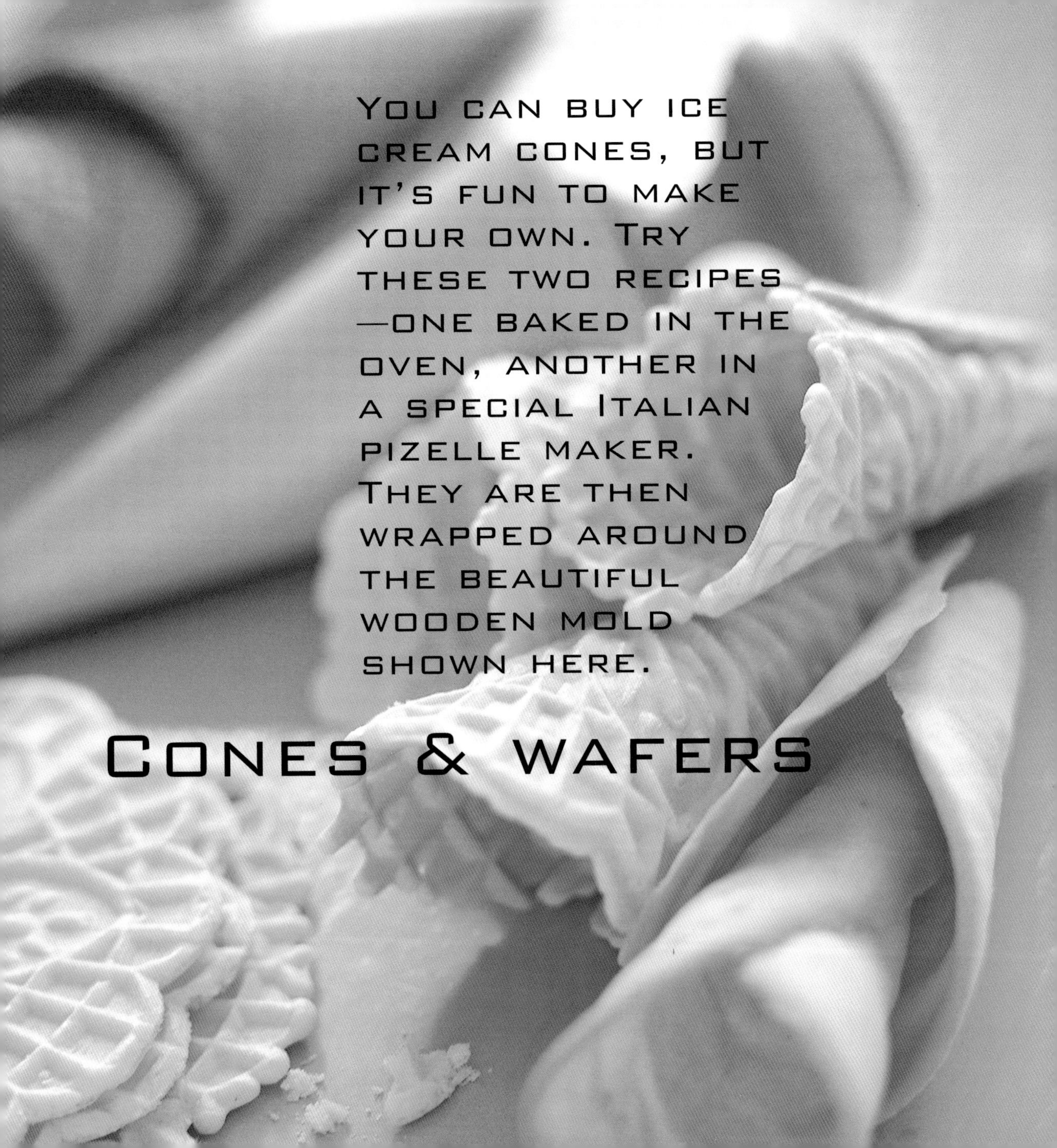

You can buy ice cream cones, but it's fun to make your own. Try these two recipes —one baked in the oven, another in a special Italian pizelle maker. They are then wrapped around the beautiful wooden mold shown here.

CONES & WAFERS

1¼ cups sugar

1⅓ cups all-purpose flour

3 egg whites

½ teaspoon vanilla extract

confectioner's sugar, for dusting

several non-stick baking sheets, lightly greased

MAKES ABOUT 50

YOU CAN BUY ICE CREAM WAFERS—EITHER RECTANGULAR OR FAN-SHAPED—OR YOU CAN MAKE YOUR OWN LIGHT AND AIRY LADY FINGERS.

Mix the sugar and flour in a food processor. Put the egg whites in a bowl and, using an electric mixer, beat until stiff peaks form. Add the vanilla, then fold in the flour-sugar mixture, a little at a time, until thoroughly mixed.

Put the mixture in a piping bag fitted with a ½-inch plain nozzle. Pipe 2-inch strips, spaced well apart, onto the prepared baking sheets. Dust lightly with

Lady fingers

confectioner's sugar for a crisp top.

Bake in a preheated oven at 350°F for about 12–15 minutes until the edges are lightly golden. Remove from the oven and transfer to a wire rack to cool. Store in an airtight container until ready to use.

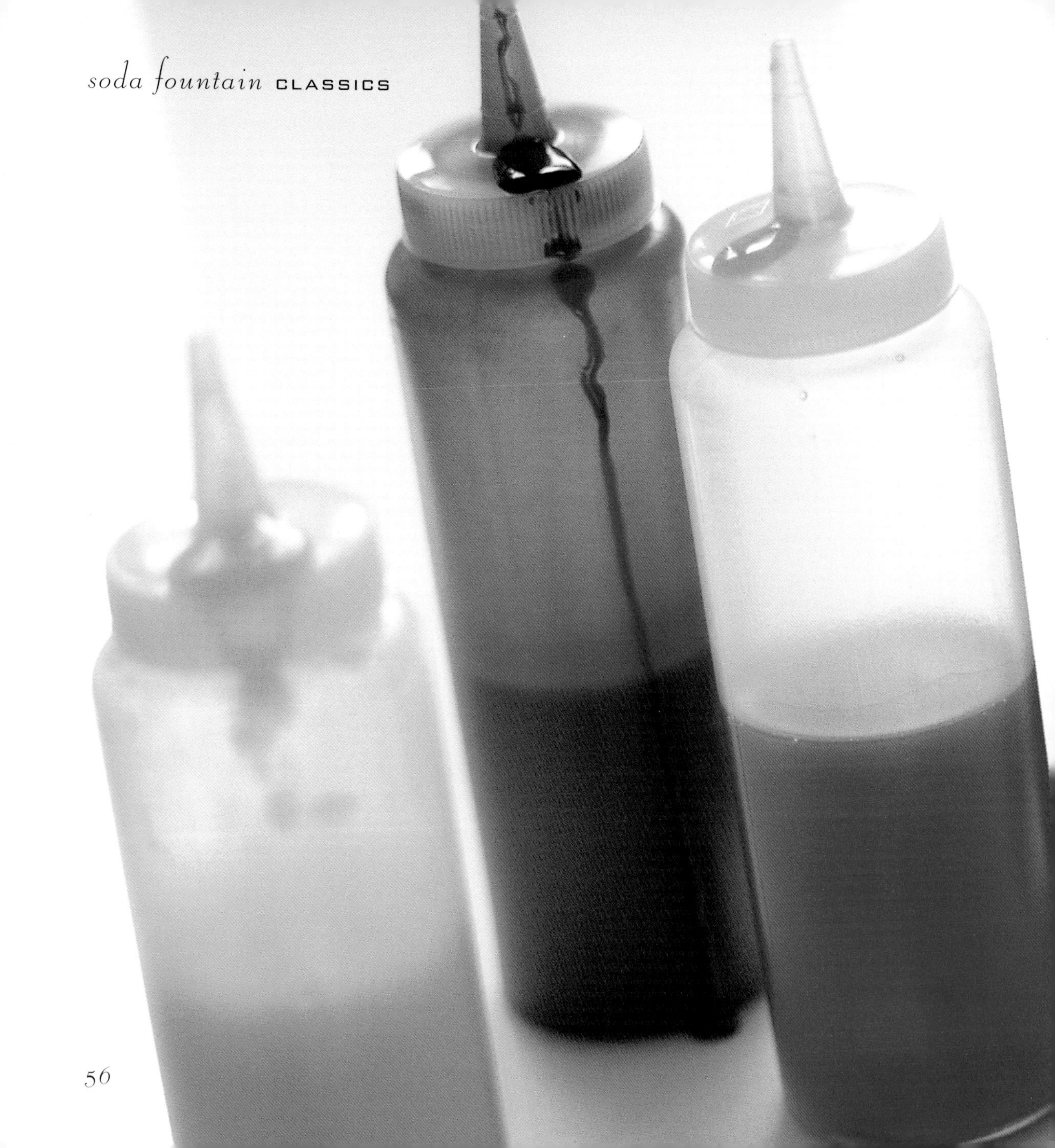

Sauces & Syrups

Soda fountain sauces and syrups are legendary, especially the chocolate ones. But these easy homemade varieties are equally delicious.

Hot rum-raisin sauce

1½ cups sugar

1 cup seedless raisins

a pinch of salt

1 tablespoon lemon juice

¼ cup dark rum

2–3 squares unsweetened chocolate

½ cup heavy cream, heated

MAKES ABOUT 3 CUPS

Put the sugar, raisins, salt, and lemon juice in a saucepan, add ⅓ cup water, bring to a boil, and simmer for 15 minutes to extract the flavor. Transfer to a blender, purée until smooth, then return to the pan and stir in the rum.

Melt the chocolate in a bowl set above a saucepan of simmering water—don't let the water touch the bowl. Alternatively, microwave at medium in short 30-second bursts (about 2 minutes in all) until melted. Stir in the hot cream, mix well, then pour over ice cream while still hot.

Hot chocolate sauce

1 cup heavy cream

¼ cup sugar

about 6 squares unsweetened chocolate, broken into pieces

MAKES ABOUT 1 ½ CUPS

Melt the chocolate as in the previous recipe. Stir the hot cream into the chocolate and mix well. Serve hot, warm, or at room temperature.

Hot fudge sauce

4–5 squares dark chocolate, chopped

2 tablespoons unsalted butter

2 tablespoons corn syrup

½ cup brown sugar

½ cup heavy cream

MAKES ABOUT 1 ½ CUPS

Put all the ingredients in a saucepan and heat, stirring, until melted. Bring to a boil, remove from the heat, and serve hot or warm.

Caramel sauce

1 cup sugar

MAKES ABOUT 2 CUPS

Put the sugar and 1 cup water in a medium saucepan and bring to a boil over medium heat. Boil hard, without stirring, until golden brown (brush crystals from the side of the pan with a pastry brush dipped in water). Add ½ cup water to the pan (take care to avoid splatters). Return to the heat and stir until the mixture dissolves. Chill, then serve as a sauce, or stir into ice cream before churning.
If using in ice cream, decrease the amount of sugar in the ice cream base, or the ice cream will not freeze hard.

Coffee syrup

1 cup freshly ground coffee

2 cups sugar

MAKES ABOUT 3 CUPS

Put the coffee and sugar in large, 12-cup French press, then fill with boiling water, about 2 cups. Stir to dissolve the sugar and release the coffee flavors. Let cool, then push the plunger, strain into a pitcher, and chill.

Honey syrup

3 tablespoons honey

3 tablespoons light corn syrup

MAKES ABOUT ⅓ CUP

Put the honey, corn syrup, and 1 tablespoon boiling water in a saucepan, bring to a boil, then pour over ice cream or waffles.

Butterscotch sauce

½ cup brown sugar

½ cup heavy cream

⅓ cup butter

MAKES ABOUT 1 ¼ CUPS

Put all the ingredients in a saucepan and stir over medium heat until melted and boiling. Reduce the heat and simmer for 3 minutes. Serve hot, poured over ice cream, or cool and chill. When cold, the sauce will set.

Note: Old-time movie theatres served ice cream in cones dipped in chocolate. To make your own, freeze the filled cones until very cold, then dip into the sauce—it will set on contact.

Pineapple syrup

1 large ripe pineapple

sugar (see method)

MAKES ABOUT 4 CUPS

Peel and core the pineapple. Cut the flesh into chunks and put into a food processor or blender. Blend until smooth, then add ½ cup sugar for every ⅔ cup pulp. Blend again. Transfer to a stainless steel saucepan, bring slowly to a boil, reduce the heat, then simmer for about 10 minutes, stirring frequently. Cool then chill. Use as a syrup, sauce, or flavoring for ice cream and sherbet.

VARIATION:

Instead of blending the fruit, put it through a juicer.

Strawberry sauce

3 baskets strawberries

1 tablespoon lemon juice

¼ cup sugar

1 teaspoon cornstarch (optional)

MAKES ABOUT 2 CUPS

Put the strawberries, lemon juice, and sugar in a saucepan and heat gently until the juices run. When the berries have become pale and the juice dark, press through a plastic strainer or simply strain the juice.
To make a thicker sauce, bring the syrup to the boil, mix 1 teaspoon cornstarch with 1 tablespoon cold water, stir into the sauce, and simmer until the syrup clears. Use as a sauce or syrup, or to flavor ice cream.

Golden fruit sauce

6 large, yellow-fleshed peaches or nectarines, or 12 apricots

1 tablespoon lemon juice

sugar (see method)

MAKES ABOUT 2 CUPS

Skin the fruit by running a sharp knife around the middle. Dip in hot water for a few minutes, then slip off the skins. Slice the fruit thinly and weigh. Measure an equal amount of sugar and put in a saucepan. Add the prepared fruit, lemon juice, and ½ cup water. Bring to a boil, simmer to form a purée, then blend until smooth, adding extra water if necessary.

Chopped nuts

2 cups mixed nuts, or single variety

Put the nuts in a dry skillet and heat gently until lightly toasted. Remove, cool, and transfer to a food processor. Pulse a few times until the nuts are coarsely chopped, then transfer to an airtight container.

Toasted coconut

1 cup shredded coconut

Put the shredded coconut in a dry skillet and heat gently, shaking the pan, until lightly toasted. Remove, cool, then transfer to an airtight container.

Chocolate curls

1 large block milk chocolate

Hold the block of chocolate in a clean dish cloth, with the long edge of the block upward. Using a vegetable or potato peeler, shave long curls off the block. Use immediately or chill on a plate in the fridge, making sure the pieces are separated so they don't stick together.

TOPPINGS

TRADITIONAL SODA FOUNTAIN TOPPINGS
WERE CRUNCHY, COLORFUL, AND
DELICIOUS. THESE DAYS, YOU CAN STILL
BUY THEM—AND MANY MORE.
TRY JIMMIES, CHOCOLATE SPRINKLES,
OR OTHER TOPPINGS YOU CAN MAKE
YOURSELF, LIKE EASY CHOCOLATE CURLS,
OR PAN-TOASTED CRUSHED NUTS OR
COCONUT. PRALINE AND FINELY CRUSHED
NUT BRITTLE ARE ALSO EASY TO MAKE IN
A FOOD PROCESSOR.

INDEX

conversion charts

Weights and measures have been rounded up or down slightly to make measuring easier.

VOLUME EQUIVALENTS:

American	Metric	Imperial
1 teaspoon	5 ml	
1 tablespoon	15 ml	
¼ cup	60 ml	2 fl. oz.
⅓ cup	75 ml	2½ fl. oz.
½ cup	125 ml	4 fl. oz.
⅔ cup	150 ml	5 fl. oz. (¼ pint)
¾ cup	175 ml	6 fl. oz.
1 cup	250 ml	8 fl. oz.

WEIGHT EQUIVALENTS:

Imperial	Metric
1 oz.	25 g
2 oz.	50 g
3 oz.	75 g
4 oz.	125 g
5 oz.	150 g
6 oz.	175 g
7 oz.	200 g
8 oz. (½ lb.)	250 g
9 oz.	275 g
10 oz.	300 g
11 oz.	325 g
12 oz.	375 g
13 oz.	400 g
14 oz.	425 g
15 oz.	475 g
16 oz. (1 lb.)	500 g
2 1b.	1 kg

MEASUREMENTS:

Inches	Cm
¼ inch	5 mm
½ inch	1 cm
¾ inch	1.5 cm
1 inch	2.5 cm
2 inches	5 cm
3 inches	7 cm
4 inches	10 cm
5 inches	12 cm
6 inches	15 cm
7 inches	18 cm
8 inches	20 cm
9 inches	23 cm
10 inches	25 cm
11 inches	28 cm
12 inches	30 cm

OVEN TEMPERATURES:

°C	°F	Gas
110°C	(225°F)	Gas ¼
120°C	(250°F)	Gas ½
140°C	(275°F)	Gas 1
150°C	(300°F)	Gas 2
160°C	(325°F)	Gas 3
180°C	(350°F)	Gas 4
190°C	(375°F)	Gas 5
200°C	(400°F)	Gas 6
220°C	(425°F)	Gas 7
230°C	(450°F)	Gas 8
240°C	(475°F)	Gas 9